# THE BOY FRIEND

Sandy Wilson was born in 1924 at Sale, Cheshire.
Education and the war had to be surmounted (the first
at Harrow and Oriel College, Oxford; the second in
the Royal Ordnance Corps, serving in Great Britain,
Egypt, and Iraq) but at the first opportunity he gravi-
tated to the theatre. While at Oxford he wrote three
revues for the Oxford University Experimental Theatre
Club and after taking his degree in English Literature
he went to the Old Vic Theatre School on a production
course. In 1943–9 he contributed material for Hermione
Gingold's *Slings and Arrows* and Laurier Lister's
*Oranges and Lemons*; in 1949–50 he contributed to club
theatre revues and wrote lyrics for Jack Waller's
*Caprice*; in 1951–2 he wrote two revues for the Watergate
Theatre, *See You Later* and *See You Again*. *The Boy Friend*
for the Players' Theatre came in 1953. He has since
written two more musicals, *The Buccaneer* (1955) and
*Valmouth* (1958), as well as songs and music for both the
theatre and television. Sandy Wilson is the author of
*This is Sylvia*, *Who's Who for Beginners*, *Prince What Shall
I Do* and *The Poodle from Rome*.

*Oh, do tell us about him, Polly!*

SANDY WILSON

# THE BOY FRIEND

*A Play in Three Acts*

\*

With a Preface by Vida Hope
*and*
Illustrations by the Author

PENGUIN BOOKS

Penguin Books Ltd, Harmondsworth, Middlesex
Penguin Books Australia Ltd, Ringwood, Victoria, Australia

—

First published by André Deutsch Limited 1955
Published in Penguin Books 1959
Reprinted 1972

—

Made and printed in Great Britain
by Hunt Barnard Printing Ltd, Aylesbury
Set in Monotype Baskerville

'The Boy Friend' was originally presented at the Players' Theatre on 14 April 1953. The first public presentation was at Wyndhams Theatre on 14 January 1954, when the cast was as follows:

| | | |
|---|---|---|
| HORTENSE, *a French Maid* | | *Violetta* |
| MAISIE | *Pupils at* | *Denise Hirst* |
| DULCIE | *Mme Dubonnet's* | *Maria Charles* |
| FAY | *Finishing School* | *Joan Gadsdon* |
| NANCY | | *Juliet Hunt* |
| POLLY BROWNE | | *Anne Rogers* |
| MARCEL | | *Stephen Warwick* |
| PIERRE | | *Jack Thomson* |
| ALPHONSE | | *Geoffrey Webb* |
| MADAME DUBONNET | | *Joan Sterndale Bennett* |
| BOBBY VAN HUSEN | | *Larry Drew* |
| PERCIVAL BROWNE | | *Hugh Paddick* |
| TONY | | *Anthony Hayes* |
| LORD BROCKHURST | | *John Rutland* |
| LADY BROCKHURST | | *Beryl Cooke* |
| GENDARME | | *Hugh Forbes* |
| A WAITER | | *Alan Dudley* |
| PÉPÉ | *Speciality* | *Stephen Warwick* |
| LOLITA | *Dancers* | *Joan Gadsdon* |
| GUESTS | | *Stella Chapman* |
| | | *Eleanor McCready* |
| | | *Robert Hargreaves* |

The part of Percival Browne was taken over in May 1954 by Fred Stone

PRODUCED BY VIDA HOPE

Dances arranged by John Heawood

Scenery and costumes by Reginald Woolley

# PREFACE

WHEN a 'miracle' show occurs, usually not more than once in a decade or even longer, people are inclined to have lengthy post mortems and ask why. Why is it such a success? The only other 'miracle' shows *I* remember are *Journey's End* – a small play with unknown actors that suddenly seized London by the throat and then went on to grip the entire world, and *Oklahoma* – the American musical which began life in a Boston theatre as an 'intimate' show (forecast by the press there as a failure) and then proceeded to rocket round the universe and change the entire shape and form of light musical entertainment. Now has come *The Boy Friend*, gaily playing to capacity in London and New York as I write these words, and due to open shortly in most of the major cities in other continents as well. Why? What makes it so successful? As the person most closely associated with it apart from the author, I'm afraid the answer is I just don't know. I have theories of course, but frankly I am not at all sure that they are right. Like the audiences in the theatre I just fell in love with it and remained in love.

When Sandy asked me to write this preface for him, I asked him what sort of thing I should write, and he said in his shy way 'I think people would like to know how we did it.' So here, then, is the answer to his request.

Early in 1953 my very good friends the Players' Theatre asked me if I would produce a new small musical by Sandy Wilson, and having accepted I went round to Sandy's flat one bleak February morning to look at the book and hear the music. He was no stranger to me as I had already produced a late-night revue that he had written previously, and we had found we got on well together. He looked pale, seemed over-anxious that I should like it, and, as always when he is nervous, played his own composition shockingly. But never mind; I saw, I heard, and I was conquered. Over coffee I declared my love for *The Boy Friend*, told Sandy I wanted to do it as a serious reproduction of a period and not a burlesque, and from that moment on his whole demeanour brightened and a friendship was forged that has withstood all the vicissitudes of the various productions of the show.

We started rehearsing in March, and I well remember haranguing a rather young company that we were to present a show that would be witty, elegant, charming and tender, and that in no circumstances would I tolerate any attitude of laughing at the Twenties. They listened politely, then went away and had their lunch, when no doubt they expounded on the lunacy of their producer and their crack-brained author. But it worked, and within less than a week the cast were even more in love with the show than we were, and were telling each other off for any hint of over-playing or burlesque business.

We all did a tremendous amount of research. My mother, who was an actress, gave me the exact formula for make-up in that era; the cast found old books of photographs and fashion drawings; and the Players' Theatre management, charming and considerate as always, produced for me some copies of *Play Pictorial* – a monthly magazine of the Twenties which gave a complete pictorial record of the successes of that time such as *No No Nanette* and *Mercenary Mary*. From these invaluable photographs I took my groupings for the ensemble work, and the girls in the show were taught stance, posture, gesture and so on. Reggie Woolley designed the most entrancing sets and costumes, all of which helped us really to 'live' the period again. I asked for John Heawood to do my choreography. He was not then known as a dance director, but I knew him as an old friend and fabulous dancer himself with a sense of style in hitting a step of the period that is almost matchless. So imbued with our show were we, that inspiration started coming, it seemed as if by magic. For instance when the hero and heroine sing 'A Room in Bloomsbury' in Act 2, I suddenly took it into my head that they should do a repeat chorus without singing the words, but in mime. This is always one of the hits of the evening, and stars like the delectable and witty Binnie Hale have asked me how I *knew* – that was what they *always* did in such a number. Well, how *did* I know? I cannot claim any credit for it – it just happened.

There were two things I was very grateful for. One was the unfailing help and complete and utter freedom the Players' management gave me. And the other was Sandy himself. He very rarely came to rehearsals, unless I particularly asked for him. His implicit trust and faith in me to carry out his intentions in a proper manner was something I shall always treasure. We seemed to have a most extraordinary *rapport* over *The Boy Friend*, which remains to this day. It is not unusual in the theatre for author and producer to be justifiably suspicious of each other and have their little quarrels over interpretation or presentation, but over *The Boy Friend* – never. We both knew what we were aiming at and we have watched over the child from birth, Sandy as father and mother, and myself as some old auntie who gets the child ready for the party.

When the final dress rehearsal arrived, we were in more of a flutter than is customary. Not only was there the usual flurry, with nerves and disturbances (we had an undue amount of illness during rehearsals – at one period the entire cast had German measles but manfully worked on – as we *all* had it there was no question of infecting others!), but we were all so dizzy with love for our show, that we couldn't bear the possibility of anyone not liking it. But all was well – they *did* like it, and the rest is theatrical history that needs no further explanation.

So that is the story of how we did it. And here for you to read is the very play I saw that February morning. I wonder will your reaction be the same as mine? I think it will, for here in Sandy's writing is a tenderness that catches the heart as well as the period dialogue that seems so funny and fatuous to present-day audiences. And added to that are his delightful sketches to embellish it.

I am delighted that Sandy asked me to write the preface to his book; partly because we have been so closely associated over this show, and partly because I can now record in black and white my gratitude to every single person connected with the original production, all of whom gave much more than was asked or necessary to their individual jobs or performances.

But perhaps the chief reason for my pleasure is that the creation of *The Boy Friend* in the theatre gave me some of the greatest thrills and fun in my life.

Thank you, Sandy.

                                        VIDA HOPE

# THE BOY FRIEND

## ACT I

The Drawing Room of the Villa Caprice, Madame
Dubonnet's Finishing School, near Nice – Morning

## ACT II

The Plage – That Afternoon

## ACT III

The Terrasse of the Café Pataplon – The same night

TIME: 1926

As I look through this published version of *The Boy Friend*, I am reminded of an observation made by Noel Coward in the preface to his *Collected Sketches and Lyrics*. He said that, while the sketches made reasonably good reading, some of the lyrics might appear rather baffling, divorced from their tunes, but he assured his readers that 'Although they may not appear to scan on paper, they scan all right when fitted to the music.' May I echo Mr Coward with reference to the lyrics included in this book? To some of its readers I hope a few of the melodies may be familiar, but I would like to crave the indulgence of those who have not seen the show and suggest, as Mr Coward did, that they make up their own tunes!

The question I am most frequently asked about *The Boy Friend* is: 'How did you know, at your age, what the shows of the nineteen-twenties were like?' In fact I believe that people who have not met me imagine I am three old men. The truth is that, although only an infant at the time, I was surrounded by elder sisters and their friends who were constantly learning the Charleston and playing 'Tea for Two' and 'Lady be Good' on an old cabinet gramophone. In fact I used to refuse to go to bed until one of my sisters had played me the record of a song entitled 'Do Shrimps Make Good Mothers?' As I grew older and the twenties gave way to the thirties, I still looked back on the period with great fondness and I can clearly recollect, while at my prep school, trying to remember how the tune of the Charleston went. Later on, at least five years before *The Boy Friend* was thought of, I would lose no opportunity of seeing touring revivals of nineteen-twenties musicals and buying sheet music of the period at second-hand music dealers. So by the time the Players' Theatre asked me to write the show, there was no need for research. I seemed to know all about it, and everything came tumbling out on paper as if it had been waiting to be written.

The fact that so many other people seem to look upon the period of *The Boy Friend* with the same fondness as myself, regardless of their age, has given me enormous pleasure. But I would like to make it clear, here and now, that this show was never intended as a 'reply to *Oklahoma*' or indeed to any of the very successful and essentially modern American musicals. I feel that the English Theatre has very far to go before it can rival Broadway in this field. *The Boy Friend* is simply a loving salute to those far-off days of the cloche hat and the short skirt, a valentine from one post-war period to another. To write it, to see it come to life, and to watch it achieve success was for me a wonderful and, I believe, unique experience.

SANDY WILSON

# ACT ONE

# ACT ONE

¶ *The Drawing Room of the Villa Caprice, Madame Dubonnet's
Finishing School on the outskirts of Nice. At the back, french
windows opening on to the garden, with a view of the sea beyond.*

*As the curtain rises* HORTENSE, *a chic French maid, is on
the phone.*

### HORTENSE

'Allo, 'allo! Is that Monsieur Gaston, the costumier? 'Ere
is Madame Dubonnet's maid. Dubonnet. D–U–B–O–N–
N–E–T . . . Madame Dubonnet of the Villa Caprice, the
school for young ladies . . . I wish to know if you 'ave ready
the costume for Miss Polly Browne. Browne. B–R–O–W–
N avec E . . . with an E . . . she wishes it for the carnival ball
ce soir. . . .

*The door L. flies open and in rush* MAISIE, DULCIE, FAY,
*and* NANCY; *four extremely pretty girls in summer frocks
and hats. They carry dress and hat boxes and are in a state of
extreme animation.* HORTENSE *rings off.*

### HORTENSE

Mam'selles! Mam'selles! Silence, s'il vous plait! 'Ave you
forgotten who you are?

### THE GIRLS

Forgotten who we are? Of course not!

We're perfect young ladies
Preparing to take
Our places among the noblesse.

We're perfect young ladies
Preparing to make
The most of the charms we possess.

We're being finished,
And our families' wealth
May be diminished,
But at least we all have perfect health.

And making the grade is
Our duty, you see,
For perfect young ladies are we.

\*     \*     \*

We're perfect young ladies
Who hope to attract
A husband whose credit is good.

HORTENSE

You may be young ladies,
But why don't you act
The way that a young lady should?

I've often told you –

GIRLS

Please don't tell us again.

HORTENSE

I ought to scold you –

GIRLS

But you know it
Would be quite in vain.

For being our maid is
Your duty, you see . . .
For perfect young ladies are –

HORTENSE

Perfect young ladies. Hm!

GIRLS

Perfect young ladies are we.

*In the course of the number* HORTENSE *relieves them of their boxes and* EXITS. *The number ends and the girls giggle excitedly.*

DULCIE

Oh, I can't wait for this evening! My frock is a dream!

FAY

So is mine! And rather daring too! I'm sure Madame Dubonnet will be furious!

MAISIE

Not she! I bet you she'll turn up in something frightfully shocking! [*They all laugh*]

DULCIE

Do you think we shall be allowed out late?

MAISIE

Who cares? I intend to dance the whole night through!

FAY

Do you, Maisie? Who with?

MAISIE

Anyone who asks me!

DULCIE

Don't take any notice of her, girls. She'll dance all night with Bobby van Husen, that terribly rich and good-looking American who's staying at the Negresco! [*Laughter*]

MAISIE

Oh, no, I shan't. He bores me! [*She goes to the windows*]

NANCY

Oh, isn't she the limit!

DULCIE

No wonder they call her Madcap Maisie!

MAISIE

Oh, look, here comes Polly Browne, across the tennis court.

FAY, DULCIE, and NANCY

Polly Browne?

MAISIE

Yes. She's carrying a letter. [*She waves*] Hullo, Polly!

FAY, DULCIE, and NANCY

[*Joining her*] Hullo, Polly!

POLLY ENTERS. *She is a sweet girl in a simple frock with no jewellery. She carries a letter.*

POLLY

Oh, hullo everyone! Where have you been?

MAISIE

We dashed into town to get our costumes for the Carnival Ball! We couldn't wait until Monsieur Gaston delivered them!

FAY

You must see mine, Polly! You'll adore it!

DULCIE

And mine! You'll be green with envy!

MAISIE

Oh, be quiet, chaps. You know we'll all be jealous of Polly when she gets hers. What are you going as, Polly?

POLLY

I'm going as Pierrette.

FAY, DULCIE, MAISIE, and NANCY

Pierrette! How divine!

MAISIE

Now do tell us your secret, Polly.

POLLY

What secret?

MAISIE

Well, if you're going as Pierrette, who's going to be Pierrot?

POLLY

Oh – I still want it to be a secret.

THE GIRLS

Oh, Polly!

POLLY

But – I've had another letter. From Paris.

FAY

From Paris! How marvellous!

POLLY

[*Reading letter*] He says he's motoring down overnight; in fact he should be here any moment now.

DULCIE

Oh, how thrilling!

FAY

And how does he sign himself? Does he say 'Passionately yours'?

MAISIE

Or 'Yours adoringly'?

DULCIE

Or does he just say 'With all my love'?

THE GIRLS

Oh, do tell us about him, Polly!

#### POLLY

Well, there really isn't very much to tell. I expect you
know how I feel as well as I do ...

Any girl who's reached the age
Of seventeen or thereabouts
Has but one desire in view.
She knows she has reached the stage
Of needing one to care about;
Nothing else will really do.

#### DULCIE

Childhood games are left behind,

#### FAY

And her heart takes wing,

#### MAISIE

Hoping that it soon will find

#### GIRLS

Just one thing.

#### POLLY

We've got to have
We plot to have
For it's so dreary not to have
That certain thing called the Boy Friend.

#### POLLY and GIRLS

We scheme about
And dream about
And we've been known to scream about
That certain thing called the Boy Friend.

### POLLY

He is really a necessity
If you want to get on.
And we might as well confess it, he
Is our *sine qua non*.

### POLLY and GIRLS

We sigh for him
And cry for him
And we would gladly die for him
That certain thing called the Boy Friend.

ENTER BOYS *centre stage through french windows.*

We plead to have
We need to have
In fact our poor hearts bleed to have
That certain thing called the Boy Friend.

We'd save for him
And slave for him
We'd even misbehave for him
That certain thing called the Boy Friend.

### BOYS

Life without us is quite impossible
And devoid of all charms.
No amount of idle gossip'll
Keep them out of our arms.

### POLLY and GIRLS

We're blue without
Can't do without
Our dreams just won't come true without
That certain thing called the Boy Friend.

DULCIE

Boys, boys, you know you're not allowed on the premises!
You must leave at once! [BOYS EXEUNT] But you still
haven't told us much about him, Polly!

FAY

Not even his christian name –

NANCY

What is it, Polly?

POLLY

Well, it's er – it's er –

MAISIE

Cave, girls, here's Madame Dubonnet.

ENTER MADAME DUBONNET R. *She is a striking-looking lady in her forties, severely but smartly dressed. She carries a bouquet and single rose.*

#### MME DUBONNET

Tiens! Tiens! mes enfants! This is no way to behave. Away all of you to your classroom! Mademoiselle Alice is waiting to instruct you in petit point.

#### THE GIRLS

Oui, Madame Dubonnet. [*They curtsey and* EXEUNT, POLLY *going last*]

#### MME DUBONNET

Mam'selle Browne!

#### POLLY

Yes, Madame Dubonnet?

#### MME DUBONNET

I wish to have a little word with you, ma petite. Will you close the door?

#### POLLY

Yes, Madame. [*She does so*]

#### MME DUBONNET

Do not be frightened, ma chère. You have done nothing wrong. I simply wish to ask you if you are coming to the Ball tonight?

#### POLLY

Oh! yes, of course. I've ordered my frock. I'm going as Pierrette.

MME DUBONNET

So? You have a friend to take you, hein?

POLLY

Oh, yes. I had a letter today. He's arriving by car from Paris. [*Holding up letter*]

MME DUBONNET

[*Taking the letter*] From Paris, you say?

POLLY

Y-yes. From Paris.

MME DUBONNET

Then why is this letter postmarked from Nice?

POLLY

Nice! Oh! Oh dear! [*She brings out a hanky*]

MME DUBONNET

[*Returning the letter*] Do not worry, little Polly. Your secret is safe with me. Voilà! But just tell me one thing.

POLLY

Y-yes, madame?

MME DUBONNET

How does it happen that one so sweet and charming as you has to pretend to have a – how do you say? – boy friend and write herself love letters?

POLLY

It's because of my father, madame.

MME DUBONNET

Your father, hein?

POLLY

Yes. You see, when he dies, I shall be really extremely wealthy and he thinks that every man who makes advances to me is just after my fortune.

MME DUBONNET

So he forbids you to have a boy friend?

POLLY

Well – practically.

MME DUBONNET

So you invent him?

POLLY

Y-yes, I'm afraid so.

MME DUBONNET

I see. Poor little rich girl! Well, I too have had a letter today – from your father. He is coming here this morning.

POLLY

Daddy? Coming here?

MME DUBONNET

Yes. He has been to Toulon on business. When he comes I will have a little word with him.

POLLY

He won't listen.

### MME DUBONNET

Ah, well, we will see. Now dry your eyes and go to your class.

MAISIE ENTERS *through french windows.*

### MAISIE

Oh, excusez moi, madame. Je n'avais pas aucune idée que vous êtes ici.

### MME DUBONNET

That is all right, Mademoiselle Merryweather. I was about to go .[*To* POLLY] Soyez gaie, ma petite, and trust in me.

*She* EXITS.

### MAISIE

What was she saying to you, Polly?

### POLLY

Oh, nothing. My – my father's coming here today.

### MAISIE

Your father? What a thrill! Is he handsome as well as being rich?

### POLLY

You wait and see.

*She* EXITS *laughing.*

### MAISIE

Oh, wait for me, Polly! I've left my dorothy bag here somewhere. Where on earth can it be?

*She starts searching.* BOBBY VAN HUSEN APPEARS *at the french windows. He is very good-looking, wears a blazer, flannels and co-respondent shoes. He sees* MAISIE, CREEPS IN *and places his hands over her eyes. She gives a little squeal.*

BOBBY

Guess who?

MAISIE

Bobby! You're crazy to come here! If Madame Dubonnet found out, I would be asked to leave under a cloud!

BOBBY

Oh, she won't find out. I came in the back way.

MAISIE

Well, you must leave at once. Anyone might come in and find us here together.

BOBBY

I'm not leaving here before I make you promise one thing.

MAISIE

Oh, and what is that, may I ask?

BOBBY

Oh, you know as well as I do.

MAISIE

Do I?

BOBBY

Of course you do. I want you to promise to dance every dance at the ball tonight with me.

MAISIE

That's out of the question.

BOBBY

Oh, come on Maisie, be a sport. You know there's no one
else I want to dance with but you.

MAISIE

Really? I don't believe it.

BOBBY

Listen baby, to my plea;
Won't you come dancing with me?
Be my baby and say yes.
Or else I'm done for, I guess.

MAISIE

To dance with you is thrilling to
My poor ego.

BOBBY

So, baby, say you're willing to
Shake a leg.
Oh,

Won't you Charleston with me?
Won't you Charleston with me?
And while the band is playing that
Old vodeodo,
Around we will go,
Together we'll show them
How the Charleston is done.
We'll surprise everyone.
Just think what Heaven it's going to be
If you will Charleston, Charleston with me.

## Won't you Charleston with me?

With bounce

Lis - ten__ Ba - by__ To my__ plea. Won't you come

danc - ing with me_____ Be my__ Ba - by__

And say__ Yes Or else I'm done for I guess____

To dance with you is thrill - ing to my poor E - go

So, ba - by, say you're will - ing to shake a leg, oh

REFRAIN Charleston

Won't you Charles - ton with me?____ Won't you__

Charles - ton with me?____ And while the

band is play - ing that Old Vo - de - o - do A - round we will

go To - geth - er we'll show them How the__

Charles - ton__ is done____ We'll sur - prise ev - 'ry

one____ Just think what hea - ven__ It's going to

be If you will Charles - ton__ Charles - ton with me.

MAISIE

Won't you Charleston with me?
Won't you Charleston with me?
And while the band is playing that
Old vodeodo,
Around we will go,
Together we'll show them
How the Charleston is done.
We'll surprise everyone.

BOTH

Just think what Heaven it's going to be
If you will Charleston, Charleston with me.

*At the end of the dance* BOBBY *kisses* MAISIE.

MAISIE

Someone's coming!

BOBBY

I didn't hear anybody.

MAISIE

I did. You must leave at once.

BOBBY

O.K. But don't forget: I'm your dancing partner tonight.

MAISIE

Well, perhaps. I'm not promising anything.

BOBBY

You don't have to. I'm telling you! Good-bye!

MAISIE

Good-bye! Oh, he's gone! Bobby, Bobby, wait for me.

*He* EXITS *through the french windows. She* EXITS *as* HORTENSE ENTERS *followed by* PERCIVAL BROWNE, *a pompous elderly English gentleman.*

HORTENSE

I will tell Madame Dubonnet you are 'ere, Monsieur Browne. Your hat?

PERCIVAL

Thank you.

*She* EXITS. PERCIVAL *examines the room.* ENTER MADAME DUBONNET. *On seeing* PERCIVAL *she starts slightly, then controls herself.*

MME DUBONNET

How do you do, Monsieur Browne. I am Madame Dubonnet.

PERCIVAL

How do you do, Madame. I hope you will forgive this visit at such short notice; but I thought that while I was in the South of France I should visit my daughter's school.

MME DUBONNET

Quite so, Monsieur. I am so pleased to meet you. We are all so fond of Polly. Asseyez-vous.

PERCIVAL

Ah, yes. A sweet girl. Takes after her poor mother. Wish I could see more of her, but I'm so taken up with business, you know.

##### MME DUBONNET

Yes. I understand, Monsieur. But I am sure you would not put it before your daughter's happiness.

##### PERCIVAL

Polly's happiness? But she's perfectly happy, isn't she? She never complains in her letters.

##### MME DUBONNET

Oh, no, I am sure she does not. But there are certain things, Monsieur, which a young girl cannot discuss by post.

##### PERCIVAL

Oh? Such as what?

##### MME DUBONNET

Her heart, Monsieur.

##### PERCIVAL

Am I to take it, Madame, you are referring to love? I sincerely hope that nothing of that sort is allowed to occur in your school.

##### MME DUBONNET

[*Laughing*] No, no. I do not encourage it on the premises, but – well, les jeunes filles seront les jeunes filles, n'est-ce pas?

##### PERCIVAL

I don't follow you, Madame.

##### MME DUBONNET

Surely you have not forgotten all your French, Monsieur Browne – or should I call you mon petit Percy?

### PERCIVAL

What! [*Recognizing her*] Good heavens! It can't be – !

### MME DUBONNET

Mais oui, mon cher, it is. Do you not remember – your little Kiki!

### PERCIVAL

Kiki. This is impossible! Most awkward – !

### MME DUBONNET

But this is no way to greet an old friend! After all we have been to each other? Have you forgotten Armistice night in Maxims, when you – ?

### PERCIVAL

Yes, Madame, I have. Completely forgotten!

### MME DUBONNET

But surely not, chéri! I wore a red dress, and – you were
in uniform. I called you my Tiny Tommy, and we drank
champagne. Later on we danced and the orchestra played
a waltz which was all the rage in Paris. Let me see, how
did it go?

> I still recall so tenderly
> The night when first we met
> The memory's so dear to me,
> So how can you forget?
>
> Fancy forgetting
> The love that we knew
> When we were fancy free.
>
> Fancy forgetting
> What I said to you
> And what you said to me.

### PERCIVAL

> Though the years go by
> And our youth is gone,
> Memories don't die,
> Like a song they linger on.

### BOTH

> So just when I thought you'd remember it too,
> Fancy, just fancy you forgetting.

*At the end of the number,* MME DUBONNET *is about to
kiss* PERCIVAL.

### PERCIVAL

Kiki! [*Noise of girls, off* L.]

## Fancy forgetting

Valse lente

I still re-call so ten-der-ly The night when first we met ___ The me-mo-ry's so dear to me So how can you for-get? ___

CHORUS

Fan-cy for-get-ting The love that we knew When we were fan-cy free. ___ Fan-cy for-get-ting What I said to you, And what you said to me. ___ Tho' the years go by, And our youth is gone Mem-o-ries don't die, Like a song they lin-ger on, So just when I thought you'd re-mem-ber it too, Fan-cy, just fan-cy you for-get-ting. -get-ting. ___

MME DUBONNET

Ah, the young ladies have finished their classes for this morning. Would you care to accompany me round the school, Monsieur Browne?

PERCIVAL

Yes. Of course, by all means.

MME DUBONNET

Allons. This way . . . mon petit chou!

PERCIVAL

Oh!

THEY GO OUT. ENTER L. *the* GIRLS *and* POLLY, *laughing and talking.*

DULCIE

Girls, I know. Let's go and try on our costumes before luncheon!

FAY

Yes, let's!

MAISIE

Are you coming too, Polly?

POLLY

Oh, no, I think I'll just stay here. I'm expecting Daddy any moment.

DULCIE

And aren't you expecting *him*?

POLLY

Him? Oh – oh, yes, of course. [GIRLS *giggle*]

MAISIE

Let's leave her, girls. She wants to be alone.

FAY

All right. Bye-bye, Polly!

POLLY

Good-bye!

*The* GIRLS EXEUNT. *Music.* POLLY *takes out her letter, looks at it sadly, then tears it up. She goes to the window, then turns away with a sob and sits down.* TONY APPEARS *at the window. He wears the uniform of a messenger boy and carries a dress box.*

TONY

[*Coughing*] Er – excusez-moi!

POLLY

[*Turning*] Oh! You startled me!

TONY

I'm sorry, Miss. I'm afraid I came in the wrong way. This is the Villa Caprice, isn't it?

POLLY

Yes.

TONY

Well, I have a package here for Miss Polly Browne.

POLLY

Really? How funny!

TONY

Funny? Why?

POLLY

Because I'm Polly Browne.

TONY

Well, it's a very pretty name.

POLLY

Oh, thank you.

TONY

And you live up to it.

POLLY

Oh!

TONY

I'm sorry, Miss. I'm afraid I'm forgetting myself. Here's your package.

POLLY

Oh, thank you.

TONY

If you don't mind my saying so, it's an awfully pretty dress.

POLLY

Yes, it is, isn't it?

TONY

Yes, I'm sure that you – I mean it will be the prettiest at the Ball.

POLLY

Oh, I don't expect so really.

TONY

I do. In fact I know it. I –

POLLY

Yes?

TONY

Well, perhaps I'd better be going.

POLLY

Oh, yes. Oh, no. Oh, yes, perhaps you had. [*He turns to go*] I say!

TONY

[*Turning back*] Yes?

POLLY

You're – you're English, aren't you?

TONY

Yes, as a matter of fact, I am.

POLLY

You don't seem like a messenger boy somehow.

TONY

Don't I? Well, to tell you the truth, I don't usually do this
sort of thing, but just at the moment I'm afraid I'm rather
on my beam ends.

POLLY

Oh, what a shame! And at Carnival Time too.

TONY

Yes, it is a pity, isn't it? I was hoping I'd be able to go to
the Ball tonight. I'll be watching.

POLLY

Will you?

TONY

Of course. [*A pause*]

POLLY

Why don't you come too?

TONY

Me? Come to the Ball?

POLLY

Yes. Why not? I've got an extra ticket and – oh dear, you
must think me terribly forward.

TONY

No, I don't. I think you're terribly –

POLLY

Yes?

TONY

I don't claim that I am psychic,
But one look at you and I kick
Away every scruple
I learnt as a pupil
In school, my dear.


POLLY

I'm not one to make predictions,
But I've thrown off all restrictions
And don't mind confessing
I think it's a blessing
That you are here.


TONY

Though I'm prepared to find I'm wrong,
I've got a funny feeling we belong
Together.
I could be happy with you,
If you could be happy with me.


POLLY

I'd be contented to live anywhere,
What would I care,
As long as you were there!


TONY

Skies may not always be blue


POLLY

But one thing is clear as can be

## I could be happy with you

TONY

I know that I could be happy with you,
My darling.

BOTH

If you could be happy with me.

POLLY

Then you will come to the Ball?

TONY

Well, I'll try. I'll have to see about a costume.

POLLY

There's a Pierrot's costume at Gaston's. Couldn't you
borrow it?

TONY

Well, I'll see. How can I let you know?

POLLY

Let me think. I'll be on the Plage at three o'clock this
afternoon – beside the bandstand.

TONY

Three o'clock, beside the bandstand. Good-bye till then!

POLLY

Good-bye! [*He* EXITS] And I don't even know his name.

RE-ENTER MADAME DUBONNET *and* PERCIVAL.
*Simultaneously the* GIRLS *drift on.*

MME DUBONNET

Polly, I have a visitor for you!

POLLY

Oh, Daddy! [*She runs to him*] I'm so happy!

PERCIVAL

Are you, my dear? I'm very glad to hear it!

MAISIE

Has he arrived yet, Polly?

POLLY

Yes, he's arrived! He's really arrived!

*Ensemble* – THE BOY FRIEND

*CURTAIN*

# ACT TWO

# ACT TWO

¶ *The Plage. The same afternoon. The sea is in the background. Downstage is the promenade.*

*As the curtain rises the* GIRLS *and the* BOYS *are on . . . the* GIRLS *wear bathing costumes, the* BOYS *white flannels.*

### BOYS and GIRLS

What a lovely day
What a lovely day
For a dip in the sea.
Oh, what fun it will be!
Won't you come and have a swim with me?

### DULCIE

But whatever you do
When I'm swimming with you,
Please remember not to go too far.

### BOYS

Though you may look cute
In your bathing suit,
We don't know who you are.

### BOYS and GIRLS

There's no knowing
Who you are going
To meet sur le Plage.

DULCIE

You may run up against a rajah,

NANCY

Or maybe your man

DULCIE

Will be a poor man.

BOYS and GIRLS

Sal or Susie
Cannot be choosey,
For here love's a guessing game.

GIRLS

Sur le Plage.

BOYS

Sur le Plage.

BOYS and GIRLS

Everyone looks the same.

There's no saying
Who may be playing
With you sur le Plage.

BOYS

A knight who's left behind his charger

NANCY

May call you ducky.

#### DULCIE

Won't you be lucky?

#### BOYS and GIRLS

In the ocean
You'll find emotion
May play you a funny game
Sur le Plage,
Sur le Plage,
Everyone looks the same.

ENTER LORD BROCKHURST R., *a jolly English aristo-crat with a monocle and high blood pressure. He has his eye on the* GIRLS.

#### ALPHONSE

Dulcie, come along, Dulcie! Come and swim with us.

*The* BOYS *and* GIRLS EXEUNT. LADY BROCKHURST ENTERS, *gaunt and severe, with parasol.*

#### LADY B.

Hubert! Hubert! Where are you?

#### LORD B.

Oh – er – here, my dear. Just admiring the view!

#### LADY B.

So I see. So different from Bognor, isn't it?

#### LORD B.

Oh, yes, indeed! Much prettier!

### LADY B.

I'm not so sure about that, Hubert. I'm beginning to think we should have gone there in the first place.

### LORD B.

Nonsense, Hilda! Nothing like a change from routine for old people like us, I feel twenty years younger.

### LADY B.

And behaving accordingly, I notice. Really, Hubert, how can you, after our loss. [*She brings out hanky*]

### LORD B.

Now, now, Hilda, don't take on so. After all, Tony isn't dead, is he?

#### LADY B.

He might as well be. Sometimes when I think of the disgrace, I would rather he were.

#### LORD B.

Oh, come now! After all, the boy has done nothing wrong.

#### LADY B.

Nothing wrong? Disappearing from Oxford in the middle of Hilary term, ruining a brilliant career! Why, they won't even consider him for the constituency now!

ENTER DULCIE, NANCY, *and* FAY.

#### LORD B.

Well, never mind, dear. Perhaps he's found another career.

#### LADY B.

But he hasn't any money, Hubert! Not a penny to his name. Oh, dear, it gives me palpitations every time I think of it. I shall have to go and sit in a shelter.

#### LORD B.

[*Ogling the girls*] Very well, my dear.

#### LADY B.

Hubert!

#### LORD B.

Oh – er – yes, dear.

*They* GO OUT. GIRLS *giggle.*

#### DULCIE

Well, who's for a dip?

FAY

I am; are you coming, Maisie?

MAISIE

[ENTERING] Righto! How about you, Polly?

POLLY

[ENTERING] Oh, no, I think I'll just have a stroll.

DULCIE

Are you meeting *him*?

POLLY

Yes, as a matter of fact I am!

FAY

Oh, please may we stay and meet him too?

MAISIE

Don't be a ninny, Fay. Polly doesn't want us around.
[GIRLS *giggle*]

OMNES

See you later, Polly.

DULCIE

Come along, Nancy.

*They wave to her and* GO OFF. POLLY *wanders up and down looking a little anxious and glancing at her wrist-watch.* TONY ENTERS L. *He now wears a blazer and flannels. He coughs.*

POLLY

Oh! There you are!

TONY

Yes. Did you think I wasn't coming?

POLLY

Well, I – wasn't sure.

TONY

Well, you ought to have been. And I've seen Monsieur Gaston about a costume and it's all right.

POLLY

Now I shall really enjoy the Carnival Ball.

TONY

So shall I! By Jove, I never thought I should be going to it with anyone like you. It makes me feel rather nervous.

POLLY

Nervous? Why?

TONY

Well, me just a messenger boy and you a rich young lady from the Villa Caprice.

POLLY

Rich? Oh, I'm not rich. You see – I just work there as Madame Dubonnet's secretary.

TONY

Do you honestly? Then we're not so different after all.

POLLY

No.

TONY

I'm so glad. I thought you would only like the grand life –
you know, big cars, diamonds, and champagne.

POLLY

Oh, no. I'm quite content with simple things.

TONY

How ripping. So am I . . .

A life of wealth does not appeal to me at all
Do you agree at all?

POLLY

I do.

TONY

The mere idea of living in a palace is
So full of fallacies.

POLLY

That's true.

TONY

I've got a very different sort of scheme in mind,
It's just a dream designed
For two.
Would you care to hear about it, dear?

POLLY

Would I care to? Can you doubt it, dear?

## A room in Bloomsbury

Steady tempo

(He) A life of wealth does not ap-peal to me at all, Do you a-gree at all? (She) I do! (He) The mere i-dea of liv-ing in a pa-lace is So full of fal-la-cies, (She) That's true. (He) I've got a ve-ry diff-'rent sort of scheme in mind, It's just a dream de-sign'd For two. Would you care to hear a-bout it dear (She) Would I care to? Can you doubt it, dear?

REFRAIN With a quiet swing

(He) All I want is a room In Blooms-bu - ry, Just a room that will
(She) All I want is a room In Blooms-bu - ry, Just a room that will

do For you and me. One room's e - nough for us, Tho' it's on the top
do For you and me. I'll sew the cov-ers for Two old co-sy arm

floor. Life may be rough for us, But its trou-bles we'll ig - nore.
chairs. Neigh-bours will love us for We shall laugh at all our cares.

On a win-te-ry night I'll light a fire. Ev-'ry-thing I shall do As
While you're read-ing a book I'll cook a stew. Then I'll bake a plum duff E-

you de-sire. I'll be sit-ting And you'll be knit-ting And so con-tent-ed we'll
-nough for two. (Both) In our at-tic We'll be ec-stat-ic As Love-birds up_ in a

1.
be, In our dear lit-tle room in Blooms-bu - ry.

2.
tree, All we want is a room in Blooms bu - ry.

TONY

All I want is a room
In Bloomsbury,
Just a room that will do
For you and me.
One room's enough for us,
Though it's on the top floor.
Life may be rough for us,
But it's troubles we'll ignore.
On a wintry night
I'll light a fire.
Everything I shall do
As you desire.

POLLY

You'll be sitting,

TONY

And you'll be knitting,
And so contented we'll be
In our dear little room in Bloomsbury.

POLLY

All we want is a room
In Bloomsbury,
Just a room that will do
For you and me.
I'll sew the covers for
Two old cosy armchairs.
Neighbours will love us for
We shall laugh at all our cares.

TONY

While I'm reading a book

POLLY

I'll cook a stew.
Then I'll bake a plum duff
Enough for two.

BOTH

In our attic
We'll be ecstatic
As lovebirds up in a tree.
All we want is a room in Bloomsbury.

TONY

Wouldn't it be wonderful?

*At the end of the number* TONY *and* POLLY *are about to
kiss.* ENTER HORTENSE *wearing her Sunday best. She
gives a gasp of surprise on seeing* POLLY. POLLY *turns
round and sees her.*

HORTENSE

Oh, Mam'selle Browne!

POLLY

Hortense!

HORTENSE

What would Madame Dubonnet say if she saw you kissing
a young man in public?

POLLY

Oh, please don't tell her, Hortense!

TONY

Dash it all, I don't see why she should care what you do on your afternoon off.

HORTENSE

One does not take the afternoon off from being a perfect young lady, Monsieur. [*Recognizing him*] Oh, mon dieu!

POLLY

What is the matter, Hortense?

HORTENSE

Do you know who he is? He is just a messenger boy from Gaston's.

POLLY

Well, yes, I know. But he's awfully nice –

HORTENSE

If Madame Dubonnet knew that one of her young ladies –

POLLY

Please, Hortense! Let me talk to you.

TONY

Well, shall I go?

POLLY

Oh, no, Tony. I won't be a minute.

*She comes downstage with* HORTENSE.

POLLY

Dear Hortense, don't betray me. I know he is just a
messenger boy; but he is doing it because he is poor, and
I'm sure that in reality he is as well born as I am.

HORTENSE

Perhaps so. But he has no right to make advances to a
young lady like yourself in his present condition.

POLLY

But – he thinks I'm just a secretary.

HORTENSE

You told him that?

POLLY

Y-yes, I did.

HORTENSE

Hélas, quelle situation!

POLLY

Please, Hortense, don't let on to anyone. I am so happy to
have an admirer who isn't just interested in my wealth.
Surely you must know how I feel?

HORTENSE

[*Softening*] Perhaps I do. But if Madame Dubonnet should
find out –

POLLY

Oh, she won't. That is unless *you* tell her.

### HORTENSE

All right, ma petite, I give you my promise. After all, it is Carnival Time.

### POLLY

Thank you, Hortense! I shan't forget.

*[Sounds of laughter off]*

### HORTENSE

Oh, here come the other young ladies.

### POLLY

Oh, dear! Let's go, Tony. I don't want to meet them just now. They do chatter so.

### TONY

All right, Polly. Let's nip over to the promenade.

### POLLY

Good-bye, Hortense! And don't forget – ssh! You promised!

HORTENSE *waves to her.* ENTER DULCIE, FAY, MARCEL, PIERRE, *and others as required.* EXEUNT POLLY *and* TONY.

### DULCIE

I say, wasn't that Polly?

### FAY

I'm sure it was. I recognized her frock.

DULCIE

Oh, look, there's Hortense! Hortense, do tell us, was that Mademoiselle Browne with her beau?

HORTENSE

I have no idea.

FAY

Oh, yes, you have. Go on, Hortense, do tell!

OMNES

Yes, do tell. [*Etc.*]

DULCIE

Is he terribly slick and handsome?

HORTENSE

I do not know what you are talking about.

FAY

Oh, isn't she mean? If you just tell me what he's like, Hortense, I'll give you that handkerchief sachet.

DULCIE

And I'll give you those crocheted flowers.

HORTENSE

Taisez-vous, mademoiselles! It is not seemly to be so curious about a young man.

FAY

And why not? Haven't you ever been curious, Hortense?

HORTENSE

Well, I –

MARCEL

Mais oui, Hortense, I believe you have.

HORTENSE

Zut!

PIERRE

Hortense is not so prim as she pretends, eh?

HORTENSE

Oh, la la!

DULCIE, FAY, *and* NANCY

Of course she isn't! After all, she *is* French!

HORTENSE

Yes, I am. And I am very proud of it, too.

I'm often asked if I would like to travel
And visit other lands across the sea
But though it might be pleasant,
I think that for the present,
This is the place that I prefer to be.
Let others go to Sweden or Siam,
I think I'll stay exactly where I am.

They say it's lovely when a
Young lady's in Vienna,

But it's nicer, much nicer in Nice.
In Amsterdam or Brussels
The men have great big muscles,
But they're nicer, much nicer in Nice.
I've heard that the Italians
Are very fond of dalliance,
And they're also keen on it in Greece.
But whatever they may say,
This is where I want to stay,
For it's so much nicer in Nice.

### BOYS and GIRLS

She says it's nicer, much nicer in Nice
She says it's nicer, much nicer in Nice.

### HORTENSE

Some people's one desire is
To go to Buenos Aires,

But it's nicer, much nicer in Nice.
The laws are rather vague in
The town of Copenhagen,
But they're nicer, much nicer in Nice.
And some may like a flutter
In Bombay or Calcutta,
But they might have trouble with the police
    (Oh, la, la!)
Other places may be fun,
But when all is said and done,
It is so much nicer in Nice.


*The number ends with* HORTENSE *in a daring attitude supported by the* BOYS.


MARCEL

Prenez garde – Madame Dubonnet!


HORTENSE

Oh, here comes Madame Dubonnet! If she finds me like this, I shall get the – bag!


DULCIE

She means the sack!


FAY

Come along, Nancy.


EXEUNT OMNES. ENTER MADAME DUBONNET *and* PERCIVAL.


MME DUBONNET

This way, mon petit chou. The water will be as warm as toast.

PERCIVAL

Er – on second thoughts, madame –

MME DUBONNET

Why do you not call me Kiki as you used to in the old days!

PERCIVAL

All right, Kiki. But I don't think I want to bathe, after all.

MME DUBONNET

But why not, chéri? It will do you good.

PERCIVAL

I can't swim.

ENTER LORD B. *backwards.*

MME DUBONNET

Aha, I think you are telling a little fib – yes? I'm sure you can swim just like a fish – with all these big muscles. [*Pinching him*]

PERCIVAL

Oh! Kiki, don't! I'm ticklish!

MME DUBONNET

I know. I remember! [LORD B. *is fascinated*]

PERCIVAL

Someone will see!

MME DUBONNET

Who cares? This is the Riviera! Now come along, we are going to have our bathe.

PERCIVAL

But – but I haven't brought a bathing costume!

MME DUBONNET

Ça n'fait rien!

PERCIVAL

You don't mean I should bathe without –

MME DUBONNET

Non, non! But I know where I can borrow one for you. So you wait here, I will return dans un instant.

PERCIVAL

But, Kiki –

MME DUBONNET

Au revoir, mon petit poisson! [EXIT *laughing*]

PERCIVAL

Kiki!

PERCY *makes as if to follow her, decides against it. He turns back.*

LORD B.

Psst! I say! [PERCY *takes no notice*] I say, old chap!

PERCIVAL

Were you addressing me?

LORD B.

Well, I wasn't addressing the chair! Actually, old boy, I was wondering if you could help me. You seem to know your way about here – all the jolliest girls. I'm a stranger here, you see, and what's more – [*whispers*] – I've got the wife in tow. She's not a bad sort really, but – *she doesn't understand me.*

### PERCIVAL

I'm afraid I can't assist you in your domestic affairs.

### LORD B.

I don't want assistance in my domestic affairs. It's *foreign* affairs I'm talking about! Now, come on, old chap, we Englishmen abroad must stick together, you know.

### PERCIVAL

Yes, of course.

### LORD B.

Now what about this little lady you were dallying with just now? She seems a sporty little filly!

### PERCIVAL

Sporty little filly! Really, sir I must ask you to control your language. That lady is a highly esteemed member of the community.

### LORD B.

Oh, yes, yes, I'm sure she is. They manage these things so much better in France.

### PERCIVAL

She is, sir, a headmistress.

### LORD B.

I say! You are in luck, aren't you?

PERCIVAL

[*Disgusted*] Oh! [RE-ENTER MADAME DUBONNET]

LORD B.

Ah, here she comes! Now be a good fellow and introduce us.

MME DUBONNET

[*Holding up a large striped bathing costume*] Look, Percy, the latest model!

PERCIVAL

I'm sorry, Madame. I have changed my mind, I'm going straight back to my hotel.

MME DUBONNET

But, Percy, I have got you such a lovely costume. You mustn't disappoint me now.

LORD B.

Go on, old chap, do as she says. [*Raises hat to* MADAME DUBONNET *who bridles*]

PERCIVAL

I've had enough of this, I'm leaving at once.

MME DUBONNET

Are you, Percy? What have I done?

LORD B.

I say, old chap, you're upsetting her. You know that's no way to treat a headmistress! [*Laughter*]

PERCIVAL

Will you please go away?

MME DUBONNET

But, Percy, will you not introduce me to your friend. Perhaps he would like to come bathing instead, hein?

LORD B.

[*Galvanized*] By Jove, like a shot!

PERCIVAL

Kiki, this gentleman is a complete stranger to me. I've never met him before in my life.

LORD B.

But this is France, my good man. We can afford to dispenser avec les formalités, n'est ce pas? [*To* MADAME DUBONNET]

MME DUBONNET

Mais oui, Monsieur, vous avez raison!

LORD B.

I don't know what that means, but it sounds absolutely delicious.

PERCIVAL

Oh!

ENTER LADY B.

LADY B.

Hubert! Where have you disappeared to now?

LORD B.

Botheration!

LADY B.

[*Seeing him*] Hubert! Come here at once!

LORD B.

Very well, my dear. I was just asking this lady and gentleman the way to the – er –

LADY B.

Hubert! Remember we are British.

EXEUNT LORD AND LADY B.

MME DUBONNET

[*Laughing*] Oh, le pauvre petit homme!

PERCIVAL

Really, what an embarrassing situation!

MME DUBONNET

Aha, Percy, I think you were a little jealous, no?

PERCIVAL

Not at all. I just like people to behave decently, that's all.

MME DUBONNET

Just as we were beginning to enjoy ourselves!

PERCIVAL

I must have been out of my mind.

### MME DUBONNET

Oh, you are what you call a – damp blanket! You spoil all
the fun.

### PERCIVAL

It's high time you realized that things are very different
from what they were.

### MME DUBONNET

Are they, Percy? [*Vamping him*]

### PERCIVAL

Yes, most definitely.

### MME DUBONNET

Percy, Percy,
Please have mercy.
Why must you always be so sad and gloomy?
Why can't you be a little nicer to me?
Chéri, chéri,
Please be merry.
When I am trying to be bright and jolly,
It isn't nice to be so melancholy.

Oh dear,
I've got the you-don't-want-to-play-with-me blues.

### PERCIVAL

Don't-want-to-play-with-me blues.

### MME DUBONNET

It's clear
I've got the you-don't-want-to-stay-with-me blues.

#### PERCIVAL

Don't-want-to-stay-with-me blues.

#### MME DUBONNET

I am so good
At spreading mirth and joy.
But it's no good
With such a sulky boy.

I try
To play the game the other fellows all choose.

#### PERCIVAL

The other fellows all choose.

#### MME DUBONNET

I sigh
Because you always refuse.
What is a girl to do
With such a boy as you?
I've got those
Dreary
Weary
You-don't-want-to-play-with-me blues.

*At the end of the number all* EXEUNT. ENTER MAISIE
L. *and* BOBBY R.

#### BOBBY

Maisie! Maisie! Here you are at last! I've been looking
everywhere for you.

#### MAISIE

Have you? I've been for a swim with Dulcie and Fay.

BOBBY

Just Dulcie and Fay? Are you sure there wasn't anyone else with you?

MAISIE

What if there was? I can go bathing with whom I choose.

BOBBY

I wish you'd choose me.

MAISIE

I don't want to choose anyone in particular.

ENTER BOYS.

BOBBY

Why not?

MAISIE

Because I want to have a good time whilst I'm young. After all, I'm only seventeen . . .

BOBBY

But I can give you a good time. It's not as if I hadn't got plenty of cash.

MAISIE

Money isn't everything.

BOBBY

When are you going to come and see my yacht again? You liked that, didn't you?

MAISIE

Oh yes, it's a very dinky yacht. [*Waving to* MARCEL] Hullo, Marcel!

MARCEL

Mam-selle Maisie! You look ravissante! Don't forget you promised to dance the tango with me tonight.

MAISIE

Of course not!

BOBBY

But, Maisie – !

MAISIE

Oh, Pierre!

PIERRE

Mam'selle Maisie! You look enchanting. Tonight you and I will dance the two-step, yes?

MAISIE

I can hardly wait.

BOBBY

Hey, Maisie – !

MAISIE

Alphonse!

ALPHONSE

I too want to dance with you at the Ball.

MAISIE

And so you shall!

BOBBY

Maisie! Listen to me!

BOYS

Listen to all of us!

BOBBY

You're so fascinating

MARCEL

But it's aggravating

PIERRE

That you keep us waiting
To hear

ALPHONSE

Which one will be

BOYS

Your favourite he.

MARCEL

You're so very taking

PIERRE

That our hearts are breaking

BOBBY

So you should be making
It clear

BOYS

Which one of us
You rate alpha plus.

MAISIE

Now listen, boys, you should recall
I've often said I love you all.

BOYS

You love us all?

MAISIE

Yes, I love you all.
It's time you learned
That I am no fool.
Where love's concerned
I stick to this rule.

There's safety in numbers,
That's what I believe.
The girl who knows
A lot of beaux
Is never likely to grieve.
The lady who slumbers
Is left high and dry.
But I'm awake
And never miss
The chance to take
Another kiss.
There's safety in numbers
And the more the merrier am I.

*At the end of it they* ALL GO OFF. RE-ENTER POLLY
*and* TONY.

TONY

All right, Polly, the coast's clear!

POLLY

I think perhaps I'd better be getting back to the Villa. I have some letters to type.

TONY

Oh, do you have to go so soon?

POLLY

Yes, I'm afraid I must. But I'll see you at the Ball tonight, won't I?

TONY

I should jolly well think so. Where shall I meet you?

POLLY

I don't know. You say.

TONY

Well, how about the Café Pataplon at nine o'clock?

POLLY

Lovely! I shall be waiting for you.

TONY

Tonight seems a very long time away.

POLLY

It's not really. Only a few hours.

TONY

Yes, and it's going to be a wonderful evening, isn't it – Polly?

POLLY

I'm sure it is – Tony.

TONY

But it's just the first of lots of wonderful evenings –
isn't it?

POLLY

Yes – at least – I expect so.

TONY

But why shouldn't it be? Remember what you said this
morning?

POLLY

What did I say?

TONY

I could be so happy with you,
If you could be happy with me.

POLLY

I'd be contented to live anywhere.
What would I care,
As long as you were there?

TONY

Skies may not always be blue,
But one thing is clear as can be,

BOTH

I know that I could be happy with you,
My darling,
If you could be happy with . . .

POLLY

Oh, Tony! And now I really must go.

ENTER LORD AND LADY B.

TONY

[*Taking her hand*] Polly.

POLLY

Yes?

TONY

Will you – would you – kiss me good-bye?

POLLY

Yes, if you want me to.

*He kisses her.* LORD AND LADY B. *see* TONY. LADY B. *shows agitation.* TONY *sees them. Crowd begin to drift on.*

TONY

Oh, gosh!

POLLY

What's the matter?

TONY

I – I've got to hop it, Polly – quickly!

LADY B.

I tell you it *was* he, Hubert! I saw him quite distinctly.

ENTER GENDARME.

LORD B.

Are you sure, dear?

POLLY

But – but why must you go?

TONY

I can't explain now. I'll – I'll see you tonight.

POLLY

But – but – oh dear.

LORD B.

Then we must call the police. Hey, you there! Gendarme!
Gendarme!

EXIT TONY, *followed by* GENDARME

LADY B.

Gendarme! Gendarme! Stop that man!

POLLY

Calling the police! Oh, surely not! [*To* MARCEL] Oh,
Marcel, tell me quickly, who are that lady and gentleman?

MARCEL

It is the rich milor Brockhurst and his wife. They seem to
be chasing a thief.

#### POLLY

[*In soliloquy*] A thief! Oh, no, it couldn't be. And yet they are rich. And he is penniless, he told me so himself – oh dear, he must have known all along that I am not a working girl but a millionaire's daughter. Oh, dear! He's just like all the rest. [*She breaks down*]

#### DULCIE

[*Running over to her*] Polly? Did he steal something from you too?

#### POLLY

Yes, Dulcie, he did.

#### DULCIE

Not your gold bangle?

#### POLLY

Not my gold bangle. Something much more precious.

#### MME DUBONNET

[*Coming to* POLLY] What is the matter, ma petite? You look quite pale.

#### HORTENSE

[*Joining them*] I think I can explain, Madame. That man was Monsieur . . .

#### POLLY

No, Hortense! You promised!

#### MME DUBONNET

But what is it, Polly?

POLLY

It's nothing, Madame. I'm just a little disappointed, that's all. You see, I shan't be going to the Carnival Ball after all . . .

> I could be happy with you,
> If you could be happy with me.
> I'd be contented to live anywhere.
> What would I care,
> As long as you were there?

ALL

> Skies may not always be blue,
> But one thing is clear as can be,
> I know that I could be happy with you,
> My darling,
> If you could be happy with me.

POLLY *runs off in tears.*

*CURTAIN*

# ACT THREE

# ACT THREE

❡ *The Terrasse of the Café Pataplon. That night.*

*The* BOYS *and* GIRLS *are dancing.* LORD B. *is staggering around. They drink, laugh, and chatter.* ENTER HORTENSE *in peasant costume.*

### MARCEL

Voilà la belle Hortense!

### DULCIE

I say, girls, doesn't Hortense look a picture?

*They gather round her.*

### BOBBY

How many hearts are you going to break tonight, Hortense?

### HORTENSE

Taisez-vous, mon petit gars! There are ladies present.

### MAISIE

Oh, don't be so prim, Hortense! You know you'll soon be as tiddly as all the rest of us!

### FAY

I must say your get-up is terribly natty!

### HORTENSE

It is just an old peasant frock belonging to ma mère.

#### DULCIE

Hortense, do tell us. Did you see Polly before you left? Is she still determined not to come to the Ball?

#### HORTENSE

I'm afraid so. I tried to persuade her to come with me, but she said she wished to go to bed.

#### MAISIE

Oh, what a frost! Now we shall never know who her boy friend is.

ENTER MADAME DUBONNET *and* PERCIVAL.

#### PIERRE

Regardez! Regardez! C'est le père de Polly avec Madame Dubonnet.

#### LORD B.

Dubonnet? That's a familiar word! [EXIT]

#### MAISIE

Oh, doesn't she look lovely.

MADAME DUBONNET *and* PERCIVAL *come down* C. *The others* EXEUNT.

#### MME DUBONNET

Are you not glad you came to the Ball after all?

#### PERCIVAL

I'm not a bit glad. I feel such a fool in this costume.

#### MME DUBONNET

You look ravissant, mon cher – formidable! Have some champagne and then you will feel more like enjoying yourself.

PERCIVAL

I'd feel happier if I knew how Polly is. She seemed so miserable this afternoon.

MME DUBONNET

She is in love, pauvre petite!

PERCIVAL

In love? Do you honestly believe that?

MME DUBONNET

Yes, mon vieux, I do. It takes a woman to understand these things.

PERCIVAL

I'm beginning to believe you're right. Perhaps Polly misses her mother more than I realized.

MME DUBONNET

Every girl needs a mother when she is young.

PERCIVAL

I have been selfish, Kiki. I have neglected Polly. When she needed comfort, I was far away. So she turned instead to you. For that I shall always be grateful.

MME DUBONNET

It was nothing. You know, sometimes I feel as if little Polly were like my own daughter.

PERCIVAL

She could be, Kiki, she could be –

###### MME DUBONNET

What did you say, chéri?

###### PERCIVAL

I was a fool to pretend the old Percy was dead. Ah, Kiki, you are still as beautiful as ever! It seems as though time has stood still and we are once more dancing in that tiny café in Montparnasse at three o'clock in the morning.

*They dance.*

###### MME DUBONNET

Do you remember the dear old waiter with the red nose?

###### PERCIVAL

And the fat lady behind the counter who went to sleep and snored?

###### MME DUBONNET

And you said – you said you wanted the night to go on for ever!

###### PERCIVAL

Kiki, give me that champagne.

###### MME DUBONNET

So – you are beginning to remember.

###### PERCIVAL

Yes, Kiki, I am beginning to remember.

*They* EXEUNT.

BOBBY *and* MAISIE RUN ON.

MAISIE

Let's sit down, Bobby. I'm exhausted.

BOBBY

But it's early yet. I thought you said you were going to dance all night.

MAISIE

Yes, I know I did. But I'm worried about Polly. I made her promise to come to the Ball, but Hortense said she was going to bed. It does seem a shame.

BOBBY

Maybe it is. But don't worry about her. I'm the one you've got to worry about from now on.

MAISIE

Oh? And why, may I ask?

BOBBY

Because – because I want you to marry me, baby.

MAISIE

Marry you? Oh, Bobby, do you really mean it?

BOBBY

Of course I do. Will you, Maisie?

MAISIE

I don't know. You must give me time to think.

BOBBY

Well, how much time?

MAISIE

Until – until midnight tonight. I'll let you know then. I promise.

BOBBY

Okay, baby, but I sure hope the answer is yes.

ENTER DULCIE, ALPHONSE, PIERRE, NANCY, MARCEL, *and* FAY *in state of excitement.*

DULCIE

Oh, there you are, Maisie! We've been looking for you everywhere.

FAY

You must come and talk to us. We've got the most tremendous news.

MAISIE

[*Joining them*] So have I.

BOBBY

But, Maisie? What about our dance?

MAISIE

It'll have to wait. I've got to chat to my chums.

*The* GIRLS *are downstage* R. *The* BOYS *gather downstage* L.

DULCIE

Maisie, you'll never guess what's happened to us. We've been proposed to!

MAISIE

What a coincidence! So have I!

DULCIE

By Bobby van Husen? [MAISIE *nods*]

FAY

Are you going to accept him?

MAISIE

I don't know yet. I want to keep him on a string.

DULCIE

Silly Maisie.

MAISIE

Who proposed to you?

DULCIE

Alphonse!

NANCY

Pierre!

FAY

Marcel! And we haven't accepted them yet, either.

ALL

Poor boys! We've got them all on tenterhooks.

MAISIE

I told Bobby I'd let him know at midnight.

DULCIE

What a splendid notion! I say, girls, let's do the same.

FAY

Rightiho!

BF–7

###### DULCIE

Alphonse!

###### ALPHONSE

Oui.

###### FAY

Marcel!

###### MARCEL

Oui.

###### NANCY

Pierre!

###### PIERRE

Oui.

###### DULCIE, FAY, *and* NANCY

Thank you very much for your proposal. We'll let you know at midnight.

###### MARCEL

At midnight? But it is so long to wait.

###### PIERRE

They are just torturing us, ces jeunes filles.

###### BOBBY

I know. And it's not fair. Maisie, you planned this.

###### MAISIE

Well, you'll just have to put up with it, won't they, girls?

###### DULCIE, FAY, *and* NANCY

Yes!

BOBBY

Okay, so we will. But at least we can make the time pass quickly.

MARCEL, PIERRE, *and* ALPHONSE

How?

BOBBY

We can dance.

ALL

Yes!

BOBBY and MAISIE

When trouble troubles you,
The only thing to do
Is dance, you simply gotta dance.

BOYS and GIRLS

And if you've had a tiff,
You'll soon forget it, if
You dance, you simply gotta dance.
Here in the South of France
They've got a new step.
It's quite the cutest dance
Invented to step
So do step.

GIRLS

Wriggle your hips and kick up your heels,
You'll be surprised how lovely it feels.

BOYS and GIRLS

Everybody's doing the Riviera.

### BOYS

Wiggle your fingers, waggle your toes,
Just how it started nobody knows.

### BOYS and GIRLS

Everybody's doing the Riviera.
Multi-millionaires and their little pets
Do it.
Even maiden ladies who wear lorgnettes
Have taken to it.

Tell everyone to give out the news.
This is the way to shake off the blues.
Everybody's doing the Riviera.

Get on the dance floor, get in the swing,
This is the time for having a fling.
Everybody's doing the Riviera.

Clap-a your hands and slap on your thighs,
Grin like a goon and roll up your eyes,
Everybody's doing the Riviera.

### BOYS and GIRLS

All the bright young things and their bright
    young beaux
Do it.
Even duchesses and their gigolos
Have taken to it.

Ain't it terrific? Ain't it the top?
You gotta dance right on till you drop.
Everybody's doing the Riviera.

*At the end of the dance they all go* OFF. ENTER
HORTENSE.

HORTENSE

Oh! Champagne!

ENTER TONY *with parcel.* MUSIC.

HORTENSE

Oh! It is you.

TONY

Oh! [*He makes as if to go off*]

HORTENSE

Attendez! Attendez! I wish to have a word with you!

TONY

But I'm in a great hurry.

HORTENSE

You were in a great hurry this afternoon too, n'est-ce pas? Leaving poor Miss Polly without a word! Ah, les hommes, les hommes.

TONY

Er – how is Polly?

HORTENSE

Broken-hearted, pauvre petite. She refuses to come to the Ball, even though I did my best to persuade her.

TONY

Does she – does she want to see me?

HORTENSE

Who knows? But it is a pity she is not here enjoying herself in her pretty costume.

TONY

Yes, it was pretty, wasn't it?

HORTENSE

But of course if she has no partner to dance with, she might just as well stay at home.

TONY

[*Looking at the parcel*] I wonder if – but I don't suppose she wants to speak to me. She probably thinks I'm just a common philanderer. [HORTENSE *says nothing*] And yet, if you could persuade her to come to the Ball, I know I could prove that I really love her.

HORTENSE

Well, I do not know if that would be the right thing to do. But –

TONY

Yes – ?

HORTENSE

I think perhaps, in spite of all, she loves you too.

TONY

Do you honestly?

HORTENSE

So if you promise not to run away –

TONY

Oh, I do, Hortense. And merci beaucoup! Well, I'll go and change into my costume. I was just going to take it back to Gaston's, but, thank goodness, I ran into you.

HORTENSE

Do not thank me yet, mon vieux. She may not come at all.
[EXIT]

> TONY *dances with box and* EXIT. ENTER BOYS *and*
> GIRLS, *followed by* LORD B. *Laughter and gaiety in the
> course of which* DULCIE *slaps* PIERRE'S *face.* EXEUNT
> OMNES, *leaving* DULCIE *disgruntled.* LORD B. *sees*
> DULCIE *and approaches her.*

LORD B.

Er – bonsoir, ma petite!

DULCIE

Oh! You startled me!

LORD B.

Ah, you're English. I thought you were French.

DULCIE

Oh, did you honestly? Well, I'm not.

LORD B.

I didn't mean to be rude.

DULCIE

Oh, that's all right. It's just that I'm rather fed-up with France.

LORD B.

Are you? I can't imagine how a pretty girl like you could be fed-up with anything.

DULCIE

Well, I am. And not just with France. I'm also fed-up with boys.

LORD B.

With boys? Well, then, why not try something older?

DULCIE

Something older?

LORD B.

Yes, like me for instance.

LORD B.

I may be too old to run a mile.

DULCIE

Run a mile?

LORD B.

Yes, run a mile.
But there's one thing I still do very well.
I may be too old to climb a stile.

DULCIE

Climb a stile?

LORD B.

Yes, climb a stile.
But there's one thing at which I still excel.
Although my hair is turning grey,

DULCIE

Yes, it's rather grey.

LORD B.

I still believe it when I say.

DULCIE

Well, what do you say?

LORD B.

It's never too late to have a fling
For autumn is just as nice as spring,
And it's never too late to fall in love.

DULCIE

Boop a Doop, Boop a Doop, Boop a Doop.

LORD B.

It's never too late to wink an eye,
I'll do it until the day I die,
And it's never too late to fall in love.

DULCIE

Boop a Doop, Boop a Doop, Boop a Doop.

LORD B.

If they say I'm too old for you,

## It's never too late to fall in love

do it un-til the day I die And it's nev-er too late to
fid-dle that's old is more in tune And it's nev-er too late to

(Girl)                                                                  (Boy)
fall in love. Boop-a-doop, Boop-a doop, Boop-a-doop If
fall in love. Wack-a-doo, Wack-a doo Wack-a-doo The

they say I'm too old for you then I shall ans-wer
mod-ern art-ists of to-day May paint their pic-tures

"Why sir, One nev-er drinks the wine that's new, The
fast-er. But when it comes to skill I say. "You

old wine tastes much nic-er. A gen-tle-man nev-er
can't beat an Old Mas-ter." It's nev-er too late to

feels too weak, To pat a pink arm, or pinch a cheek, And it's
bill and coo. At an-y age one and one make two And it's

1   (Girl)   (Boy)   (Girl)   (Boy)
nev-er too late to fall in love. Says who? Says me. Says you, Says
nev-er too late to fall in

(Both)                2
me. Says both of us to-geth-er. It's nev-er too late to

fall in, nev-er too late to fall in love.____

DULCIE

Then I shall answer 'Why, sir,
One never drinks the wine that's new;
The old wine tastes much nicer'.

LORD B.

A gentleman never feels too weak
To pat a pink arm or pinch a cheek,
And it's never too late to fall in love.

DULCIE

Sez who?

LORD B.

Sez me.

DULCIE

Sez you.

LORD B.

Sez we.

BOTH

Sez both of us together.

LORD B.

It's never too late to whisper words

DULCIE

Concerning the ways of bees and birds,

LORD B.

And it's never too late

DULCIE

To fall in love.

BOYS and GIRLS

Whack a Do, Whack a Do, Whack a Do.

DULCIE

It's never too late to flirt and spoon,

LORD B.

A fiddle that's old is more in tune,

DULCIE

And it's never too late

LORD B.

To fall in love.

BOYS and GIRLS

Whack a Do, Whack a Do, Whack a Do.

DULCIE

The modern artists of today
May paint their pictures faster.
But when it comes to skill, I say –

LORD B.

You can't beat an old master.

It's never too late to bill and coo,

DULCIE

At any age one and one make two,

LORD B.

And it's never too late to fall in

DULCIE

Never too late to fall in

LORD B.

Never too late to fall in

DULCIE

Love.

\*     \*     \*

It's never too late to blow a kiss
Especially at a time like this

LORD B.

And it's never too late to fall in love.

DULCIE

Vodeo, vodeo, vodeo.

LORD B.

It's never too late for fun and larks,
A jolly old flame has lots of sparks,

DULCIE

And it's never too late to fall in love.

LORD B.

Vodeo, vodeo, vodeo.

DULCIE

The modern buildings that you see
Are often most alarming.

LORD B.

But I am sure that you'll agree

DULCIE

A ruin

LORD B.

Can be charming.

DULCIE

It's never too late to be a beau,

LORD B.

Experience counts a lot, you know.

BOTH

And it's never too late to fall in
Never too late to fall in
Never too late to fall in love.

*As it ends,* LADY B. ENTERS. *She sees* LORD B. *and*
DULCIE.

LADY B.

Hubert!

LORD B.

Oh, lord, the wife! [*To* DULCIE] Run along now, there's
a good girl.


DULCIE *laughs. She blows him a kiss and* RUNS OFF.

LADY B.

And who, may I ask, was that?

### LORD B.

Oh – er – just an acquaintance, my dear; we were merely passing the time of day.

### LADY B.

What, at this time of night? Really, Hubert, you are disgraceful!

### LORD B.

Disgraceful! But I wasn't misbehaving.

### LADY B.

I'm not so sure. In any case I can't think why you should wish to attend this wicked Ball, when you know how distressed I am. Our experience this afternoon has quite unnerved me.

### LORD B.

Now, now, Hilda, don't take on so. Come and sit down and I'll ask the garçon to bring a glass of port.

### LADY B.

I don't require anything to drink, thank you, Hubert. I intend to return to the hotel in a few minutes, and I shall expect you to accompany me.

### LORD B.

Very well, my dear. Just as you wish. Garçon, garçon, bring the lady a glass of port.

*The* BOYS *and* GIRLS, MADAME DUBONNET, *and* PERCIVAL ENTER.

### MAISIE

Oh, look, everybody, here comes Polly!

ENTER POLLY. *She is dressed as Pierrette and looks disconsolate.*

#### PERCIVAL

So she's come to the Ball after all. Poor child, how sad she looks.

#### MME DUBONNET

Let me talk to her, mon vieux. I know how she is feeling.

*She goes up to POLLY and leads her to a table.*

#### LADY B.

Hubert, I think that's the girl we saw with Tony this afternoon.

#### LORD B.

Are you sure?

#### LADY B.

Positive. Perhaps if we talked to her, she might be able to tell us his whereabouts.

#### LORD B.

Yes. I'll have a word with her in a minute.

#### LADY B.

No, Hubert. We'll both have a word with her, later.

#### MME DUBONNET

[*To* POLLY] Polly, you look charming.

#### POLLY

Do I, Madame?

BF–8

MME DUBONNET

But of course. You know, you were wise to come to the Ball. When one is feeling sad, the only thing to do is to try and forget.

POLLY

I shall never forget.

MME DUBONNET

Courage, mon brave. In the meanwhile, why not enjoy yourself? Look, here are all your friends around you, so do not be downcast.

*The* GIRLS *and* BOYS *surround her.*

OMNES

Hullo, Polly. [*Etc.*]

MAISIE

Hullo, Polly. I'm so glad you've come.

NANCY

We all missed you like mad, didn't we, chaps?

OMNES

Yes, we did, Polly. [*Etc.*]

POLLY

Thank you. It's so nice to know I've got some real friends.

ROLL OF DRUMS. *The* GARÇON APPEARS.

GARÇON

Attention! Attention! Mesdames et Messieurs, asseyez
vous, s'il vous plait! We now present the rage of the Con-
tinent, Pépé and Lolita, who are going to dance the
Carnival Tango.

LADY B.

Revolting!

*The assembly settle down with excited murmurs of 'The*
*Carnival Tango', 'Pépé and Lolita', etc.* BOYS *and* GIRLS
*clap.*

ENTER *the Speciality Dancers. They dance a Tango to the*
*delight and astonishment of everybody except* LADY B. *and*
GO OFF *to tumultuous applause.*

*There is a general dispersal.* POLLY *remains with* PER-
CIVAL; HORTENSE *draws* MADAME DUBONNET
*aside.*

#### HORTENSE

Madame Dubonnet, I wish to have a little word with you about Mam'selle Browne.

#### MME DUBONNET

Yes, Hortense? What is it?

#### HORTENSE

I fear she is wishing to leave the Ball already, but if you can persuade her to stay, I do not think she will regret it.

#### MME DUBONNET

Very well, Hortense, I will do what I can.

#### HORTENSE

Merci, madame.

EXIT HORTENSE. MADAME DUBONNET *joins* POLLY *and* PERCIVAL.

#### MME DUBONNET

You do not wish to dance, Polly?

#### PERCIVAL

I have already asked her myself, but she prefers not to.

#### MME DUBONNET

Never mind. The night is still young. Let you and I have a little talk together.

#### POLLY

Very well, madame.

PERCIVAL *goes upstage.*

MME DUBONNET

You know, Polly, when I look at you in that sweet costume, you remind me of a song I knew when I was a child.

POLLY

Do I? Can you sing it?

MME DUBONNET

Yes, I think so.

> There is an old French legend
> That's set to an old French tune.
> It tells how Pierrot loves Pierrette
> Under a summer moon.
> Every night the lovers meet
> Just as the clock strikes nine.
> Then he gives her kisses sweet
> As vintage wine.
> But, alas, one fateful night
> Pierrette is forsworn,
> There she stands forlorn
> Till the cold grey dawn.
>
> Poor little Pierrette,
> Where's your Pierrot?
> Why are you all alone?
> You should be
> So fancy-free.
> Your heart should be high.
> But instead
> You hang your head
> And try not to cry.
>
> Poor little Pierrette,
> You mustn't show

## Poor little Pierrette

Moderato, à l'antique

There is an old French leg-end That's set to an old French tune It tells how Pier-rot loves Pier-rette Un-der a sum-mer's moon Ev-'ry night the lov-ers meet Just as the clock strikes nine Then he gives her kis-ses sweet, As vin-tage wine But a-las one fate-ful night Pier-rette is for--sworn, There she stands for-lorn, Till the cold grey dawn.

REFRAIN With feeling, not too slow

Poor lit-tle Pier-rette, Where's your Pier-rot? Why are you all a-lone?___ You should be, so fan-cy free, Your heart should be high.___ But in-stead You hang your head And try not to cry.___ Poor lit-tle Pier-rette, You must-n't show Your dream of love has flown___ Just keep on danc-ing Till the dawn, and then

1 & 2

He may come back a-gain.

3

-gain.___

Your dream of love has flown.
Just keep on dancing
Till the dawn, and then
He may come back again.

*At the end of the number, the others* RE-ENTER. TONY
APPEARS *dressed as Pierrot and masked.* HORTENSE
*runs to* MADAME DUBONNET *and points him out excitedly. Everyone is riveted.*

#### HORTENSE

Regardez, Madame Dubonnet. C'est Pierrot. Il est arrivé!

#### MME DUBONNET

Look, Polly! Pierrot has not forgotten after all!

#### POLLY

Oh! [*putting on her mask*]

TONY *comes down looking at all the ladies. He finds*
POLLY.

#### TONY

May I have this dance, Pierrette?

#### POLLY

I'm afraid I can't dance with a stranger.

#### TONY

But I am Pierrot. You are Pierrette. Surely we are not strangers?

#### POLLY

But I don't know who you are.

TONY

Perhaps this will remind you. [*He kisses her*]

POLLY

It isn't – it isn't –

TONY

[*Removing his mask*] Yes, Polly, it's me.

POLLY

[*Removing hers*] Tony!

TONY

Polly!

LADY B.

Hubert! It's Tony! We've found him at last!

LORD B.

[*Going to him*] Tony! My boy! [*They embrace him*]

PERCIVAL

And who, may I ask, is this young man?

LORD B.

This, sir, is my son, the Honourable Tony Brockhurst.

POLLY

The Honourable Tony Brockhurst! Oh!

TONY

Yes, Polly! I'm afraid I am not a messenger boy after all.
Can you forgive me?

POLLY

Oh, yes!

LADY B.

And who, may I ask, is this young woman?

PERCIVAL

This, madam, is my daughter. And I am Percival Browne.

TONY

Percival Browne, the millionaire?

POLLY

Yes, Tony. I'm afraid I've deceived you too. I'm not a secretary after all. Can you forgive me?

TONY

Of course, my darling! [*They embrace*]

MME DUBONNET

La, la, it seems that love is in the air tonight.

PERCIVAL

It is indeed. Polly, I too have some news.

POLLY

Have you, Daddy? How thrilling!

PERCIVAL

May I tell her, Kiki?

MME DUBONNET

But of course. She should be the first to know.

### PERCIVAL

Very well, then. Polly, Madame Dubonnet has just consented to become my wife.

### BOBBY

Maisie! It's midnight – have you thought it over?

### MARCEL

Et toi?

### PIERRE

Et toi?

### ALPHONSE

Et toi?

GIRLS

After due consideration we have come to the conclusion
that the answer is unanimously – yes!

BOBBY

Swell – now how about that Charleston?

*Everybody charlestons to* THE BOY FRIEND.

GRANDE FINALE *with Balloons and Streamers.*

*CURTAIN*

*Some Penguin fiction*
*is described on the*
*following pages*

# COLETTE

## CHANCE ACQUAINTANCES

The two short novels contained in this volume vary widely in mood and treatment. *Julie de Carneilhan* is a straightforward novel of pre-war Paris, alternating between the studio of the proud but impecunious Julie and the house of her ex-husband, the Comte d'Espivant, who has recently married a wealthy widow. She is still attracted to the Comte, who makes use of her affection to improve his financial position. But the family traditions of independence free her from Parisian intrigue.

*Chance Acquaintances* is a story told in the first person. Colette goes, accompanied by her cat, to a health resort. Here she becomes involved with a married couple. Though first drawn towards the husband, it is the invalid wife who finally wins her affection. This does not prevent Colette, while on one of her business trips to Paris, from performing an errand of intrigue for the husband.

## CHÉRI and THE LAST OF CHÉRI

*Chéri* is certainly her most famous and perhaps her finest book. Chéri, brought up in the fabulous *demi-monde* of the wealthy Parisian courtesans of Edwardian days, handsome as the devil, capricious, the spoilt darling of a far from conventional set, at a tender age is handed over by his mother – 'lent' his mistress prefers to term it – to the care of her accomplished friend Léa de Lonval.

The sequel is Chéri's tragedy. A minor hero of the war, which has accustomed him to solitude, he finds it impossible to settle down to a new life among his go-getting friends. Haunted by memories of his carefree, love-lavished youth and the bounty of his benevolent mistress, he falls into a steady decline.

# NANCY MITFORD

## THE PURSUIT OF LOVE

It was inevitable that the Radlett children should display, in their later years, the habit of rebellion from convention and authority, for they were brought up in an odd home ruled by a violent and eccentric father. The little world he governed was largely devoted to killing things, and the reaction of the high-spirited Young Radletts was to go to the opposite extreme – even to the length of releasing captured animals from traps.

## LOVE IN A COLD CLIMATE

Many of the characters from *The Pursuit of Love* reappear in this book – including Boy, the remarkable Uncle Matthew, and the younger members of the Radlett family with their unquenchable curiosity, their Hons' cupboard and their exclamations. The plot is again un-folded by Fanny, daughter of the notorious Bolter, but this time it is mainly the story of Alconleigh's neighbours, the Montdore family – a wealthy, successful, and highly aristocratic couple with an only child.

## THE BLESSING

The Pursuit of Love in a foreign country is never plain sailing for a typical Englishwoman. Grace Allingham, good, beautiful, and not very clever, makes a hasty war-time marriage with Charles-Édouard de Valhubert. When he comes back from the war and takes her home to Provence her married life begins and so do her troubles. If the country in France seems complicated to Grace, life in Paris is too much for her. And her life is not made easier by the machinations of her small son, Sigi.